THE UNOFFICIAL

T0083903

COLORING BOOK

This book is unofficial and unauthorized. It is not licensed, approved, or endorsed by the writers, producers, or any affiliated associates of the *Ted Lasso* television series; Warner Bros. Entertainment Inc.; or Universal Television LLC.

Illustrated by Indira Yuniarti

Adams Media
New York London Toronto Sydney New Delhi

Adams Media
An Imprint of Simon & Schuster, Inc.
100 Technology Center Drive
Stoughton, Massachusetts 02072

Copyright © 2022 by Indira Yuniarti.

All rights reserved, including the right to reproduce this book or portions thereof in any form whatsoever. For information address Adams Media Subsidiary Rights Department, 1230 Avenue of the Americas, New York, NY 10020.

First Adams Media trade paperback edition November 2022

ADAMS MEDIA and colophon are trademarks of Simon & Schuster.

For information about special discounts for bulk purchases, please contact Simon & Schuster Special Sales at 1-866-506-1949 or business@simonandschuster.com.

The Simon & Schuster Speakers Bureau can bring authors to your live event. For more information or to book an event contact the Simon & Schuster Speakers Bureau at 1-866-248-3049 or visit our website at www.simonspeakers.com.

Illustrations by Indira Yuniarti
Soccer ball images © 123RF/tribalium123

Manufactured in the United States of America

10 9 8 7 6 5 4 3 2 1

ISBN 978-1-5072-2096-2

Many of the designations used by manufacturers and sellers to distinguish their products are claimed as trademarks. Where those designations appear in this book and Simon & Schuster, Inc., was aware of a trademark claim, the designations have been printed with initial capital letters.

This book is unofficial and unauthorized. It is not licensed, approved, or endorsed by the writers, producers, or any affiliated associates of the *Ted Lasso* television series; Warner Bros. Entertainment Inc.; or Universal Television LLC. All trademarks are the property of their respective owners. The publisher makes no claim of ownership and shall acquire no right, title, or interest in such marks by virtue of this publication.

INTRODUCTION

Welcome to the dog pound! From the stands and pitch of Nelson Road Stadium to the booths and bar of The Crown & Anchor, the world of *Ted Lasso* is yours for the coloring. It's time to break out the biscuits and colored pencils and settle in for a jolly good time.

Like an inspirational speech from the coach himself, *The Unofficial Ted Lasso Coloring Book* brings the same heart and earnest joy that won over Roy Kent and the rest of the Greyhounds. You'll get to revisit all of your favorite sights and settings from the series as you color in thirty illustrations, including:

- The stadium seats of Nelson Road
- Your very own BELIEVE poster
- Lasso's iconic visor, aviators, and whistle
- Higgins's closet office
- The Greyhounds' locker room
- And many more!

Keep calm and color on as you make your way through the wide world of *Ted Lasso*. With so much to color, you'll be as happy as a goldfish.

BELIEVE

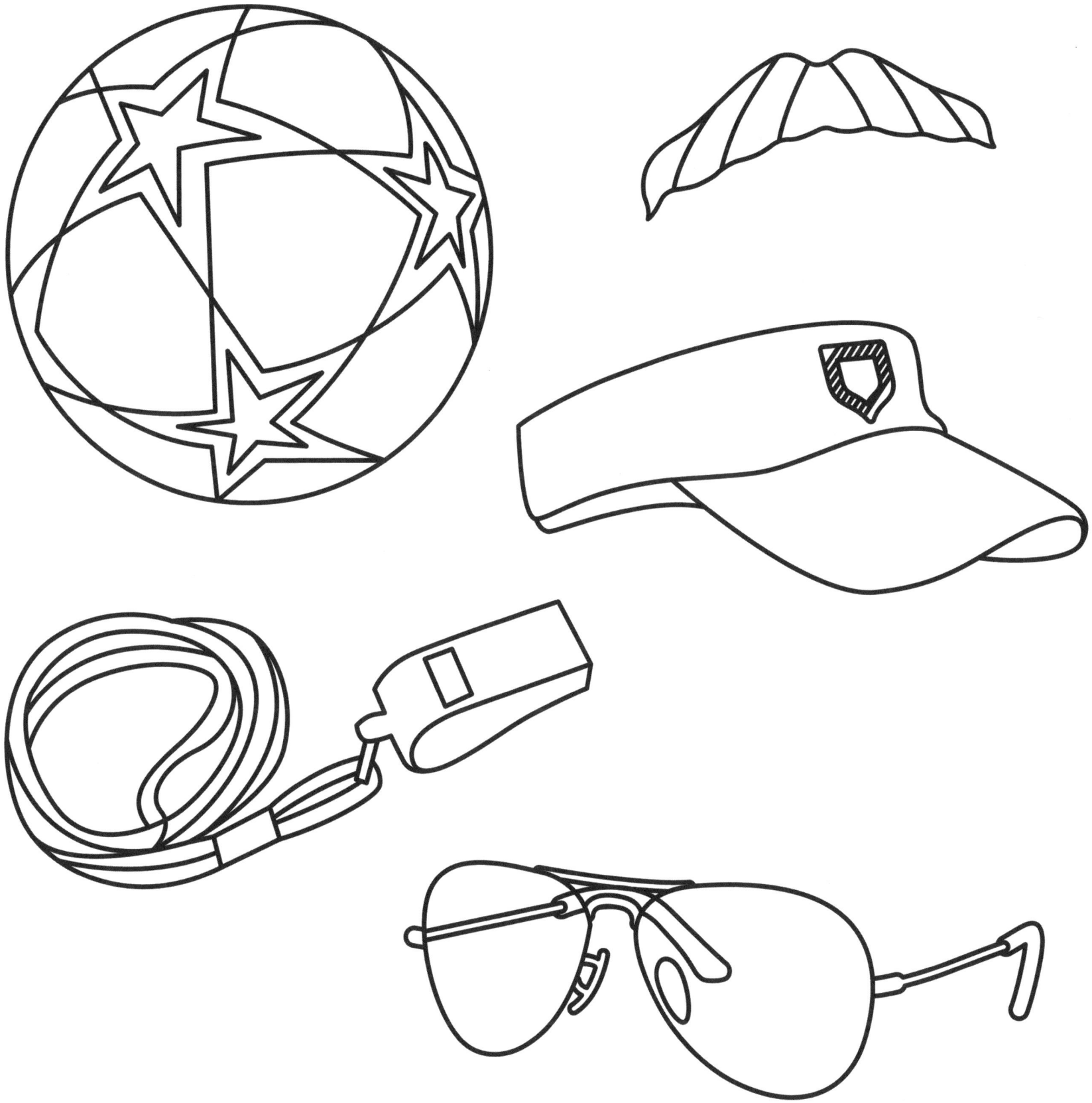

BISCUITS WITH
the Boss

Be a Goldfish

RIP EARL

PRESS

A Wrinkle
in
Time

BE CURIOUS
20
1
18
4
13
6
10
15
2
17
3
19
7
16
8
11
14
9
12
5
NOT JUDGMENTAL

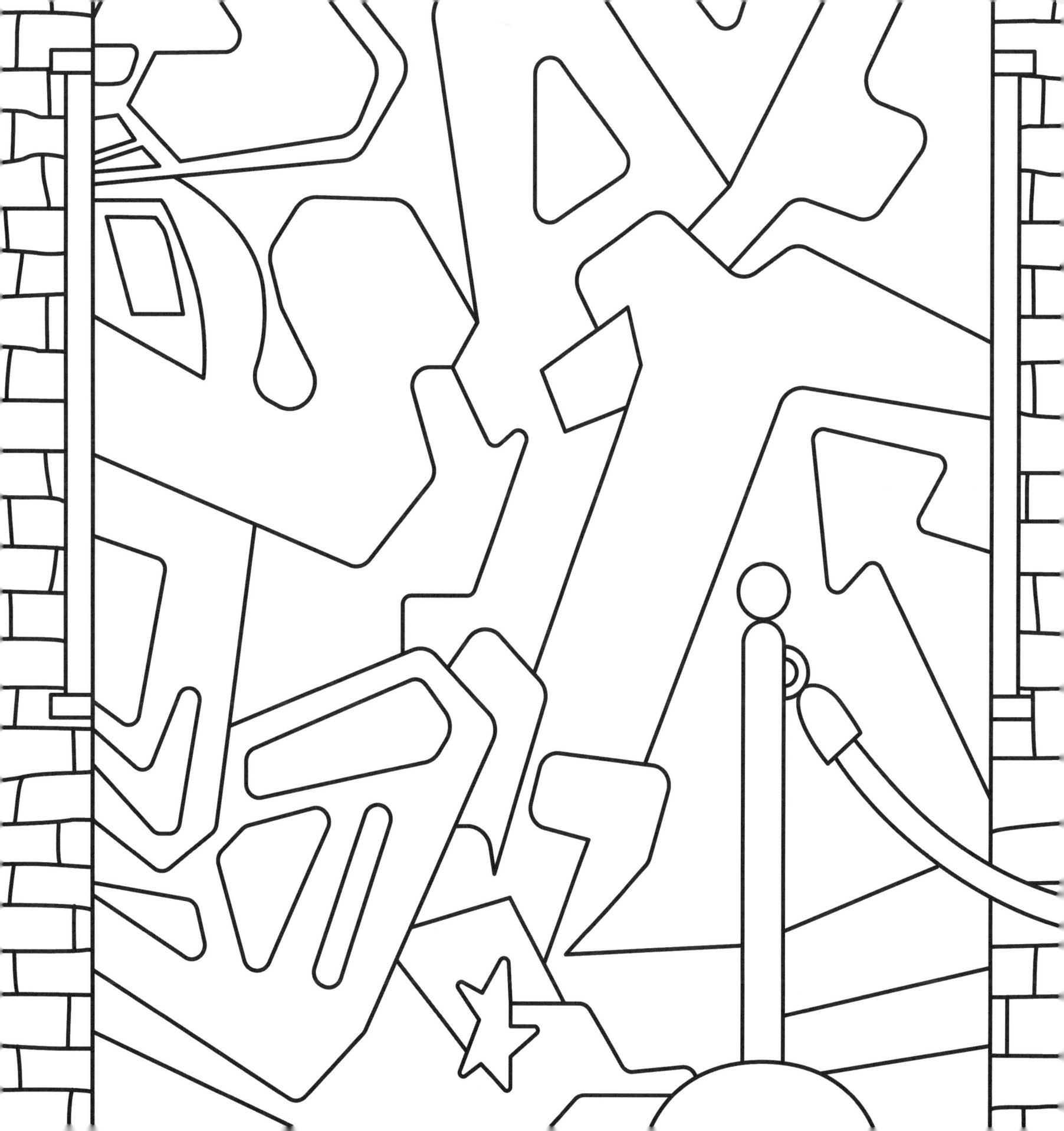

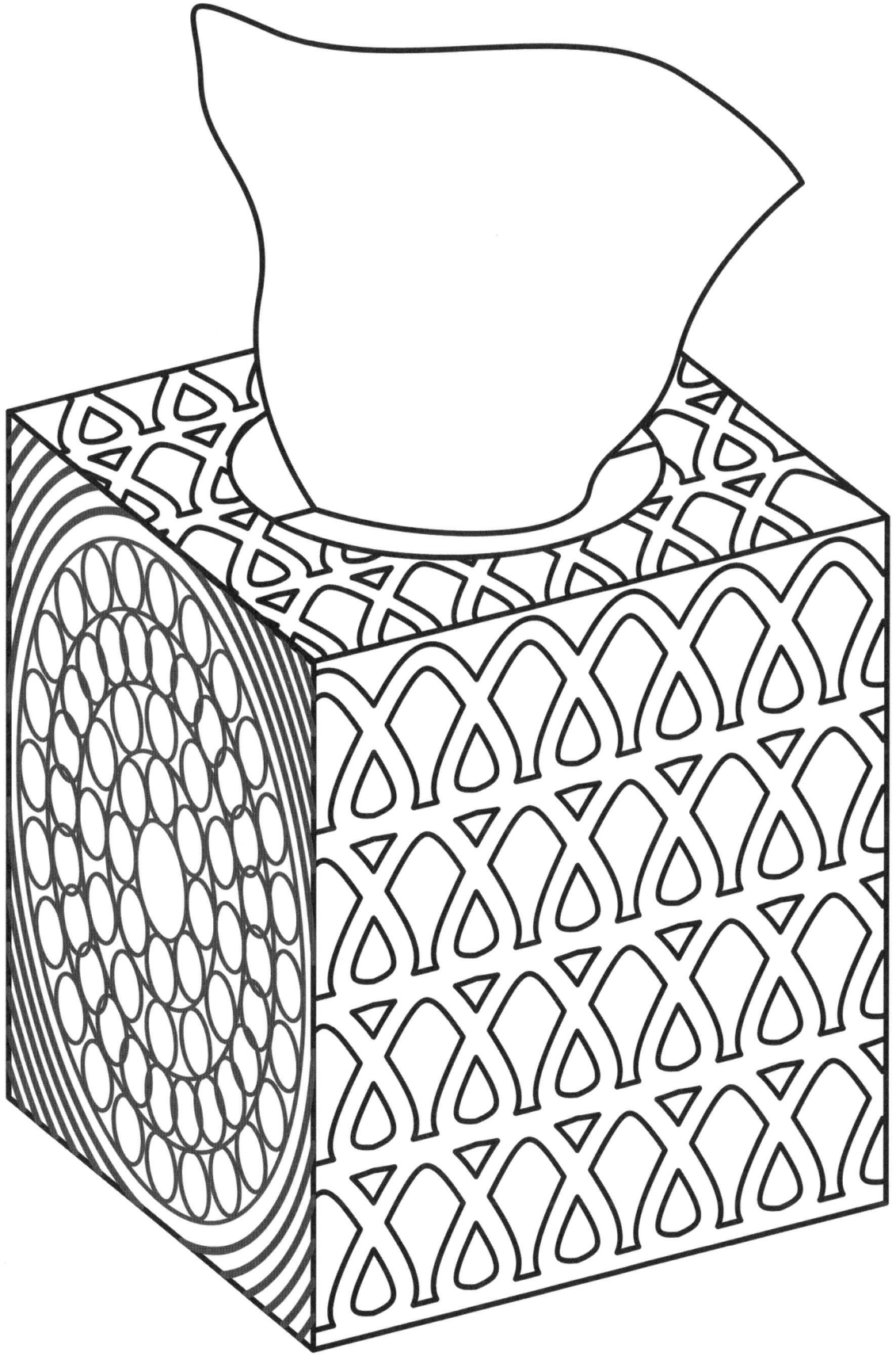

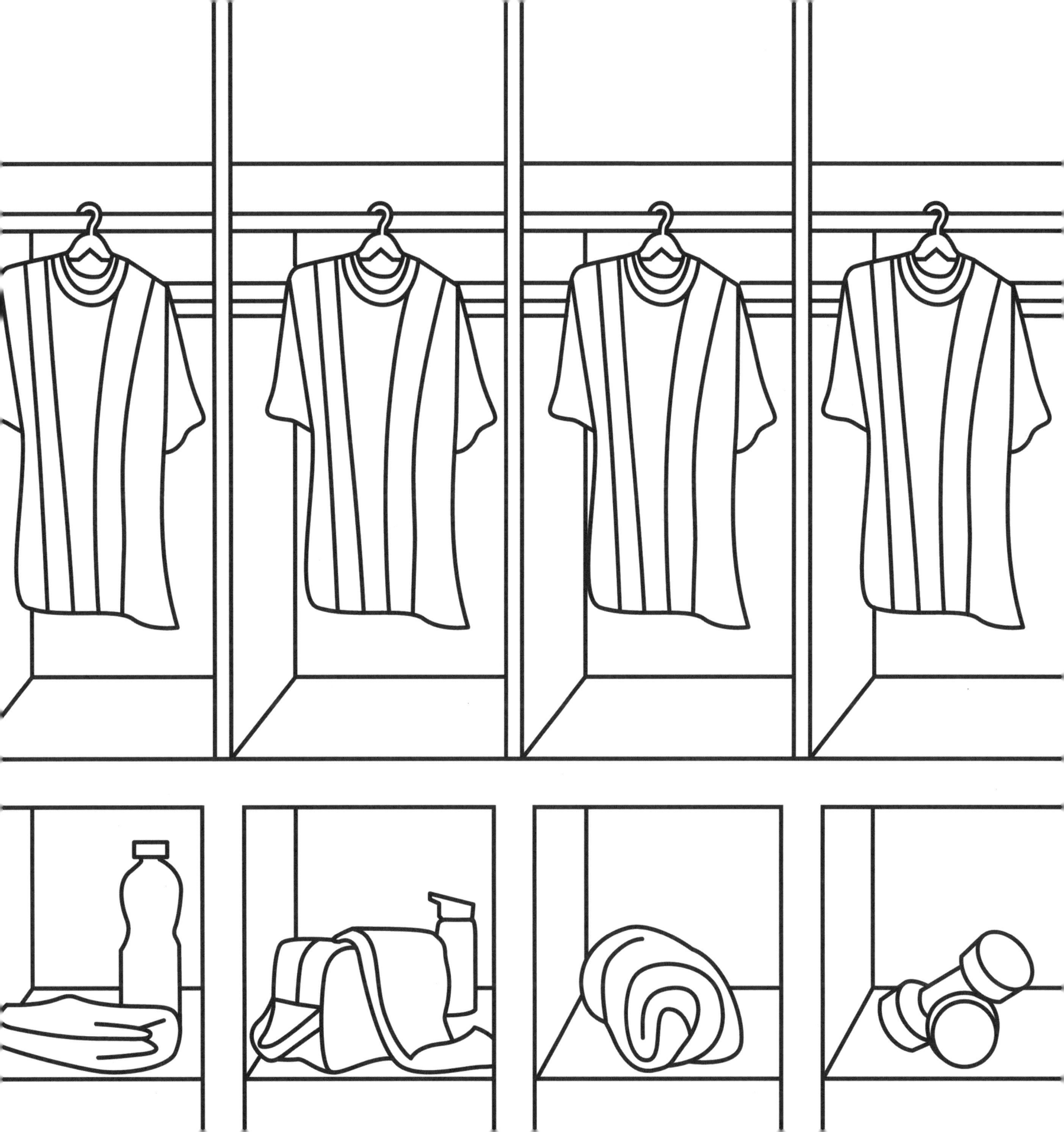

WHITEBOARD
WHITEBOARD
WHITEBOARD
WHITEBOARD

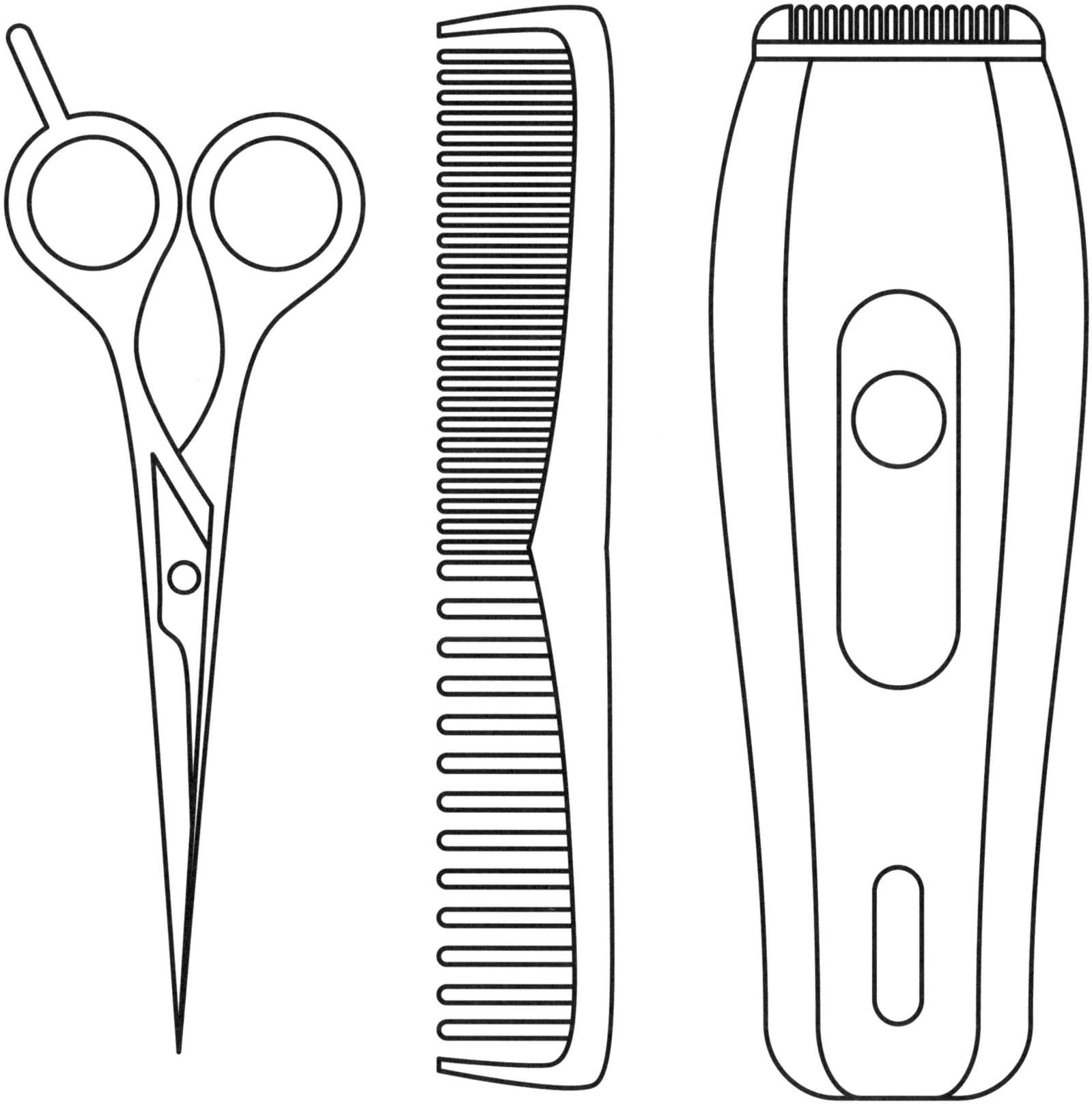

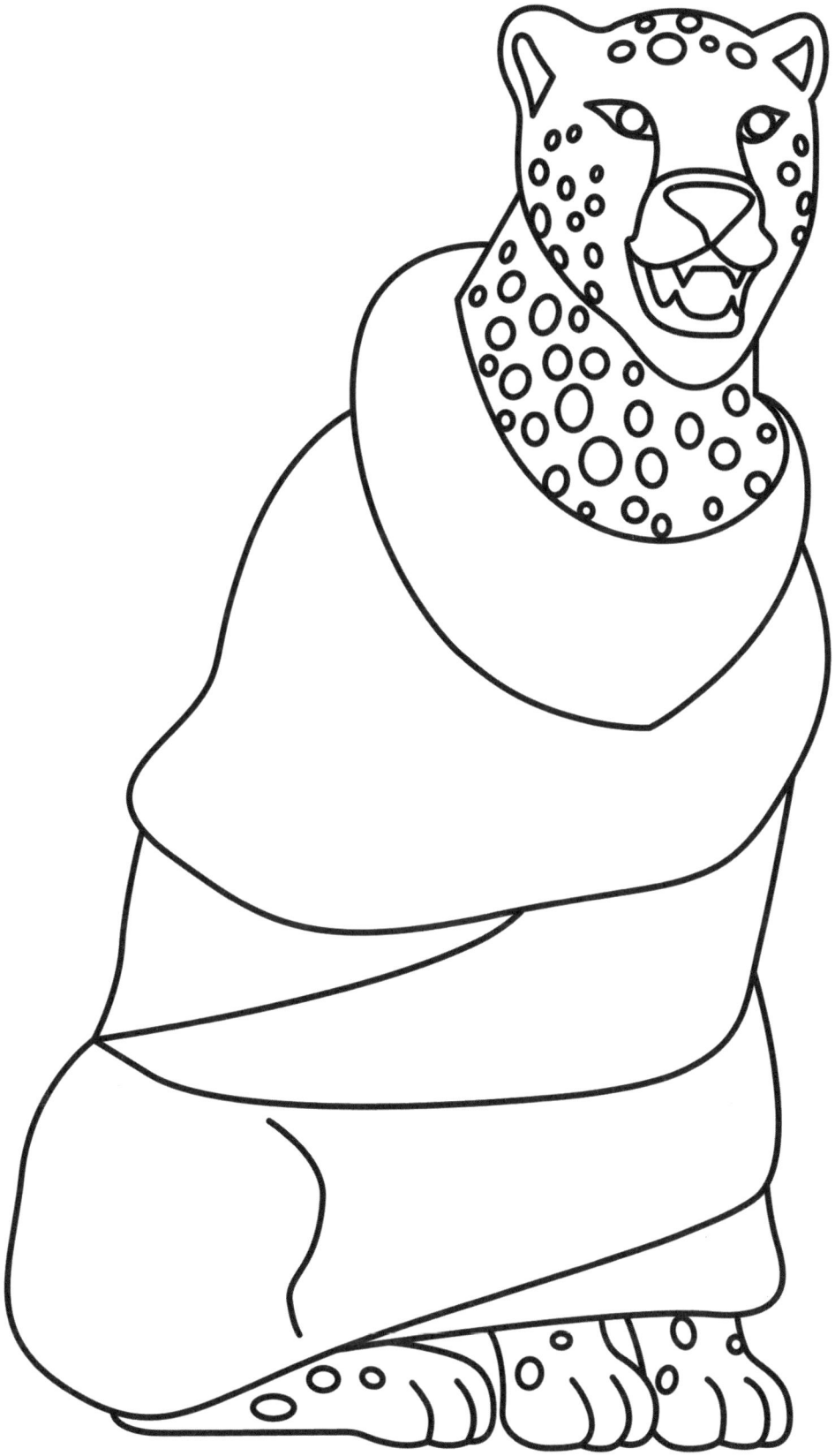